W9-BAH-117

# Alexa:

# 2017 New and Updated Tips and Tricks

Paul Laurence

ISBN: 1979863733
ISBN-13: 978-1979863735

# CONTENTS

Thank you for purchasing this book!

I hope it will be useful for you.

We always try to give more value then you expect. That's why we update the content of the digital version of the book very often and you can get it for **FREE**.

You can get the digital version of this book for free, because you bought the print version.

The book is under the match program from Amazon. You can find how to do this using next url:
**https://www.amazon.com/gp/digital/ep-landing-page**

## Introduction

Do you like Alexa? Have you ever used Alexa? Well, you're lucky. This new system is always being updated, with new tips and tricks that can help you get the most out of it. With software updates that are constantly being given to you, using Alexa to get the information that you want, to be the best personal assistant that you can get, is definitely something nice.

But what are some of the upgrades and features of Alexa? What are some of the tips and tricks that you could potentially obtain from this system? Well, you're about to find out. This book will go over the nuances of Alexa, what it means for you, and what you should be considering if you're going to get this system.

Not only that, there is a chapter here spotlighting the new hardware, the new second generation of Echo, which is essentially a better version of the original, and it comes with a whole bunch of great new features. Plus, with all that this system has to offer, you'll never miss out on anything that Alexa can tell you, which in turn will allow you to have an even better, more remunerative system that is good for you.

So what are you waiting for? What are you going to do next? Well, the best thing to do next, is to continue reading on, to learn all about what Alexa can do for you, what this system has to offer, and a whole slew of other amazing things. Alexa is in your control, and you can use it in order to truly get the benefits that you desire. Use Alexa to your advantage, and you'll soon be able to control various aspects of your home, and everything that you so desperately want to, with just your voice. It's amazing, and this book will tell you of the new updates, and the new tips and tricks that Alexa has to offer to make your smart home experience, one that's so much better.

# 1 Chapter – The New Echo (second Generation)

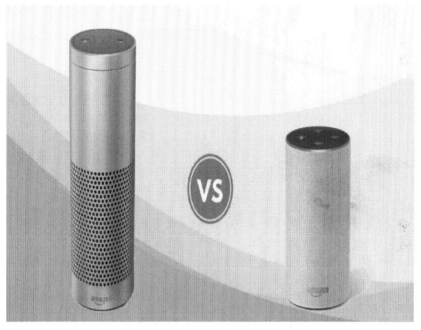

Do you live the Echo? Are you thinking about possibly getting a new one? All of these questions are something that you might have asked yourself over recent months, and you've probably seen with a lot of the new products that have come out, that one of them stands above the rest. One of the newest and best smart devices out there is the Echo system, but there were a few bugs in it. Amazon did take these into consideration, and now, with this Alexa device now updated, the Echo second generation will be out on the market during the holiday season.

What's so great about it though? After all, many have said that it's mostly the same thing, but that definitely isn't the case. It's actually the update that this system needed, especially when compared to the original Echo system, and the offshoots that were from it. It's been tested and added to, and Amazon did listen to the feedback the customers had with the original system, including the dreaded microphone problems that many of them had. Well, you're lucky, because it is a system that's been tried and true, and the best part, is that Amazon cares enough to make sure that you're getting a device that works like a charm, and a device that can be used to bring your home to the land of smart appliances. And the best part, is the fact that you're not putting down a whole slew of money on this either, meaning that you won't have to pay a lot to just get the results that you want, and the best Echo system out there. It's affordable too, which is something that many people seemed to be worried about initially when the system first came out, since it did have a much steeper price tag back then. We'll go into the in-depth analysis on this system, and why it's considered one of the best smart devices on the market.

**General pros and Cons**

It's important to understand that there are a few pros and cons on this system, and we'll go over them in a bit of a superficial manner, since this is something that is important to know about when you're choosing this.

The pros are simple: it's cheaper, smaller, has some nice design options, and some great features. If you've been holding out on getting one of these, now is the time that you should definitely consider doing so.

The main con, is well, it's not that much different from the first generation system, which isn't a bad thing, but if you're considering upgrading to this from the first generation, you might not see much of a benefit to it. The microphone, while improved as well, might not be what you totally desire, but it's certainly a step-up.

But, it's definitely a great system, especially when you think about it, there was a time when there weren't smart speakers, which is a strange concept, but of course, it's probably a strange concept as well to think about talking to some device that will do everything for you. But, it's an awesome system, and the changes that have been made were indeed, for the better.

**Evolving through the Years**

Now, Amazon has worked hard to provide you with the digital assistant revolution that we've all wanted deep down in our hearts. It started in 2014, where it was only available to those with a Prime account, but after a year it started to get a general release, and after that, it started to expand its sales to newfound territories. There are many different branches of the Echo system now, including the Dot, Tap, Show, and the recent Echo Spot. But, all of these came from this amazing first system, and it's been something that has helped those live a digital life in the way that they want to.

There are rumors of promotions on this one during the holiday season, and currently with a 100-dollar price tag, it's definitely something that could be worth the investment. After all, for less than 100 dollars, you could finally get the Alexa system in your home.

**Designed for Success**

Probably the one thing that is really great compared to the first generation, and what's totally worth it, is the size of this. Now, this is a striking feature because the first generation was a lot bigger, and a lot fatter, which is what made it hard to put it anywhere. But, thanks to the design, which has been super streamlined, and listened to by Amazon, it's definitely way more attractive than the first one. It comes with the sleek and modern design, but it also has a nice sandstone finish that is courtesy of Amazon, and it definitely is much more attractive than the original system. It looks nice, and it definitely is one that's worth the price itself.

It might seem dinkier, about 89 mm dinkier if you want the exactness of it, but it also doesn't look like a Blade Runner sort of thing. It looks way more like an Ikea device. It kind of does away with a lot of the futuristic looks that the first one had, and it doesn't look nearly as drab. The best part, is that you can get it in a ton of different colors.

If furnishing your home based on the decor of the home is important to you, you should definitely consider the options that they have here. Yes, you can get the original black and white one with the plastic finish, but if you want to get one with a certain fabric, or even a finish, you can. The following are the design options: charcoal fabric, heather gray, silver finish, sandstone fabric, oak finish, and walnut finish. There are so many for you to choose from, and this will mean for anyone who is trying to make their home the best that they can, totally possible, since this is a designer's dream.

So yes, you can customize your Echo device to your office now. A lot of times the standard might look best, but if you're truly trying to get a big array of different options to choose from, making it a step in the right direction for Echo customization, which is pretty great, and can be of immense help in truly personalizing your smart assistant if you so desire.

You can get various designs as well, but one of the things that you should definitely know about before you begin is that you can't switch these out, so make sure that you make the fitting choice before you do fork over the cash. However, you might realize that it looks so much prettier than before.

Now, another nice thing about it as well, is that if you want to add a headphone to this system, well guess what, you can put the headphones into the jack. It's right next to the power input outlet, so if you want to, you can even plug in an external speaker if you want the sound quality, or just Bluetooth enable these as well, whichever works for you.

That means that it can be put in a variety of other locations. That's what's so nice, and the fact that one can nestle it nearly on a shelf without much interference is something that is often seen as a benefit when discussing this Echo version.

It also has the same features as the one before. It's helpful because if you already have one, but you want to put another one in your home, you most certainly can. It comes with a ring at the top that signifies when Alexa is thinking of a response, listening to you, or even on. You can also see the rings whenever you receive a call or a message, which is pretty great. The buttons are also at the same place, where you can turn it up or down to toggle this. The mute button was what will stop Alexa from processing your responses, and you can turn this on for updates that will certainly help.

It's one of the best and most attractive smart home devices on the market, and if you've been thinking about getting one, but the size of it has been a deterring factor, consider the fact that since it's been streamlined design-wise, it can certainly look a lot better as well.

## Benefits of Setting Up

One of the things that is nice about it, is the fact that it's simple to put together. The first generation was definitely something that was simple too, but this one is even simpler if you already have your information put into it. You can plug it in, secure it to a WIFI network, and if you're already linked to the fitting Amazon account, that's all you have to do.

Now, the one downside to this is just like the first system, it's not portable, which means that you're stuck keeping it in a wall, or in an outlet of some sort. It would be nice to have a battery, but it's often something that isn't there, and hopefully, Amazon takes that into consideration, so that they can fix this in order to give users more time to experience it.

## Same old Game

Now, as said before, there aren't very many differences between the first generation, and the second generation, but that doesn't necessarily mean like it's a bad thing. In fact, it's actually something that's super useful to this system. It means that you can get the same Alexa features that are on other devices, enhancing the experience. Simply by saying the name Alexa and whatever command you put in, with the skills put on there, you can listen to whatever music you want, set alarms (which is one of the newer and better features of this one), get updates on your appointments, order pizza, and so much more. If you know what skills you want, you essentially can add whatever you want to this device.

And the best part? If you have the skills you enabled on your past Alexa devices, simply by linking your account to this one, the skills all transfer over to the other Alexa device, meaning that you can control everything in your home, play games, listen to various music streaming services, and so much more. It's a system that is so easy, that if you haven't ever had an Echo system before, well, guess what, now you can. It's definitely something that was put out there to help make the user experience the same, but with some neat and new features that are certainly worth shaking a stick at.

**Sounds for Success!**

One of the biggest things that was a problem with the original Echo was the sound. It was often not something that was really touched upon, and while you can listen to music, some people liked to hook up a speaker, either Bluetooth, or via a USB jack in the back, to the other speakers so that you could use them, or use their smart speakers in order to stream music and play some tunes. However, this time around, you do get a much better sound quality than before.

It's much louder too, meaning that you will be able to play this relatively easily. Now, compared to actual speakers, some might complain that it's not nearly as good, but it definitely is great and does the job well. If you want to listen to the podcast that you're in the middle of, or even play some music while you clean up your room or something, this is the way to do it. However, don't think about using it as a speaker if you're going to have some large and crazy dance party. That won't do you much good, because while it is good, you might tend to blow out the speakers.

However, what it does well with, and what it does shine on, is the microphone. The microphone is something that is super great. It's got amazing quality, which is a step-up from the old Echo system. One of the problems with the Echo system, was too many times you'd get told by Alexa that they didn't hear that, or maybe that it processed a request wrong. This is frustrating, and it can be super annoying if you're someone that wants it done right the first time. Well, guess what, the Echo second-generation allows you to get this ability, and it does it well. If you put it in another room, and you want Alexa to hear you, well, guess what, it's going to hear you and it'll be able to process the request from the other side of the room, making this a whole lot easier for you. You'd be surprised at how nice, and how simple this is, and how you can get every single query that you have answered by Alexa right away, and at a distance, or super close too.

Now, in terms of sound quality when comparing it to the Google home speaker, is that it's less bass heavy, and it's not as harsh sounding as the other, but it definitely doesn't have too much of a difference. However, the Echo second generation does have a nice set of features to it, and it does have a whole array of other great things as well.

Now, at the end of the day, it isn't a major step-up, but if you're someone that wants a better sounding speaker system, it's certainly worth the price. Plus, it comes with Dolby sound, and it's pretty great.

Now, if you have a landline as well, this is something that can totally be a benefit as well. If you have a landline, but you don't really feel like keeping the old and prehistoric phone, you can drop it, and you can use your landline via your Echo system this time around. It is pretty great, and it actually can also work with the Echo connect as well, which is an innovative and fun thing.

**Add some Routines**

Now, the routines feature on the other Echo systems was lacking in some ways, but this time around, Alexa has finally learned how to add alarms to your routines. It's a way of customizing the phrases that you want to customize. While music might not be the thing for it, if you want to set an alarm so that it goes off and plays something when you first wake up, it totally can. If you tell Alexa good night, it can even turn off the lights, the television, and even lock the door too if you have that, and it can close the garage door. If you want to say "Alexa, it's time for work," it can turn on the smart coffee maker, and even open up the garage door, making your commute better. You can really just hook this up to any smart home appliance, and it's something that is definitely nice enough for many people, and it can make your daily activities so much easier.

**Great Value for a New User**

For those that are looking to buy an Echo system, but they've been holding back on it, honestly, now is the time to jump in on it. If you want to buy it as a Christmas gift, or even just in general because you feel like you're going to get a nice speaker in it, then this is definitely for you. With the addition of the landlines, you'll be able to use this to your full advantage, and this sleek system is certainly worth the money. So yes, it can do a whole lot, and there are other features we will discuss below as well for you to take advantage of, and ones that can really take your experience to the next level. For 100 dollars, it's a great value, and you're getting access to the best platform in terms of smart home living right now, and it has some amazing features. While it's definitely going to get upgrades and various software developments in the future, it is definitely one of the best smart home assistants for the price that you're paying for it. It's one of the best appliances out there, and if you're looking to splurge, this is the way to go.

## Other Notable Features

There are a few notable features that are also a part of this new Echo system, and it's important to understand that these new features do wonders on the system.

The first, is the landlines. This is great if you have an old landline to get rid of, and plus, it gets rid of the barrier of only being able to call those that are associated with your Alexa account. Well, that connection means that you can use your landline for other purposes, and that also means that there is so much more that you can do with it.

Voice recognition is another amazing feature. Now, the Echo has always been good at this, but one of the features is that it has beam forming technology and better noise cancellation. You'll be able to detect the wake word from all around the room even when the TV is blaring.

Bluetooth speakers are now something that you can connect to this. You can create a huge surround sound system, both from Bluetooth enabled devices, and also from other Echo devices. By putting all of these together, you can from here create a huge sound library, and you'll be able to put everything together in a very nice array of different sounds.

Another neat feature is that for those that are using Alexa for smart devices, you actually don't need to remember the name of the device or the groups of devices in order to manipulate them. Simply just say the name of the device, and Alexa will control it. It makes the ability to control your home with just your voice so much easier and more possible, and you'd be amazed at the difference this makes in your overall home performance.

Spotify premium is something that in the past, used to be something you needed a skill for. But, now with the new system, you can play music streaming on this, and it isn't just in the US anymore, it actually can be played anywhere, so if you want to learn English, chances are some Spotify songs can definitely help with this. There is a free trial as well, and if you want to give it a whirl and already have an Amazon Echo, there really isn't anything stopping you.

You can also put in repeating alarms if you want to have something put in there. This is great for whenever you want to set timers for food, but also for alarms. This is something that can be super helpful if you put it in the bedroom. You can put various names to the timers, whether it be an egg timer, chicken timer, or the bedroom alarm, and you can even tell it when it should be repeated.

With this as well, you can set up so many more IFTTS as well. If you already have a few of them set up, you can add a whole lot more as well. You can even add IFTTS to the various apps that you have as well.

You also can take full advantage of the Amazon Skills Kit, which is a way to develop and create a bunch of new skills. These are compatible with the new Echo system, and if you do use these, you'll be able to make your home even smarter. If you're savvy with programming, this is a way to truly take this to the next level, and you can enable some amazing features on your device.

This chapter talked about the new Echo second generation. It's a new generation of amazing qualities that this system has to offer, and for anyone looking to use the Echo system to the most that they can, this is a great investment. It's one that comes with a lot of new abilities, but it also doesn't do much to give you the typical Echo experience. In short, if you've wanted one for a while, and you want to try the tips and tricks listed here, right now is a better time than any to get this new Echo system, since there are a lot of great things that come with it, and a whole lot that you can do as well to truly master this system too.

## 2 Chapter – Services to Enable Immediately on your Alexa Device

Now, if you for whatever reason haven't done this yet, now is the time to enable these various services. There is a lot that is to be offered here, and this chapter will go over the services that you should enable on your Alexa device, and why you should do this.

**Music player**

If you've got a new Alexa device, and you haven't done this yet, you should make sure to change the default music services that you currently have. The device is currently set to Amazon music only, which is great, but if you don't have a Prime membership, it can be limited. However, if you have Spotify, iHeartRadio, or even Pandora, you can change this to make it the default music player so that you're putting your subscription to good use. To do this, you want to go to settings, choose music and media, and then link account to Alexa. From there, you can choose to your liking what you want to have as your default player.

**Flash Briefing**

Amazon has a flash briefing, which will give you news stories at your command. It's pretty good, but sometimes, if you don't like the news that it's providing to you, you can choose what you want. You can add or subtract various news outlets depending on personal desires. To do this, you go to settings, choose flash briefing, and then choose to get more flash briefing content. Now, make sure you don't go too crazy on this, and make sure that you mix up the types of coverage given so that it's not repeating itself. If you need help, start with one site, and choose what else interests you in terms of news.

## Calendar

While Amazon doesn't have its own service yet, if you have one from iCloud, Office 365, Outlook, or Gmail, you can definitely integrate it onto your Alexa compatible device. If you use your calendar a lot, this is something that's almost integral to your life, and something that is interesting. If you want to have an easier experience with dealing with the daily grind, this is something to consider. Alexa will even tell you about any special appointments that are on that day, and you can ask Alexa to add or subtract events, or change the time on this. You want to go to the settings tab again, this time choose calendar, and then link the one that fits your needs, and follow the instructions there.

## Alexa Calling

"Alexa, call Mom."

You can make calls with Alexa, and you can place calls to the people that are in your contacts that either have the Alexa app or the device themselves. It is actually pretty helpful, especially if you want to call someone and your phone isn't nearby.

Now, some people think that it's just between one Alexa device and another, but that's actually not the case. Friends and family don't need to have a device that's Alexa enabled in order to message or call them, all they need is the app themselves. You can also use this for video chat, so if you own an Echo Show, and you want to chat with a friend, you can do so despite them not having one.

You essentially need to give permission to talk to them, and have the person download and install the app, making sure it's the latest version, and then they're given the permissions needed to have Alexa messaging put in. They're put automatically in your contacts list, and you can communicate with that device.

If they aren't your friend at some point and want to block them, you can do so from the Alexa app. It's that simple, and something worth using.

**Family profiles**

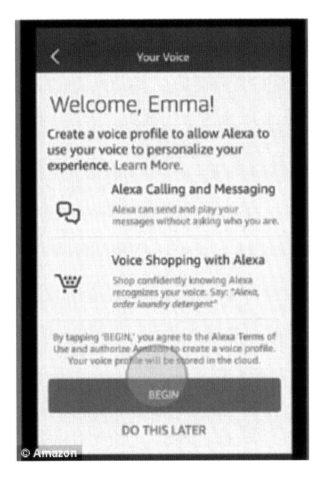

If you haven't set this one up already, then I highly suggest that you do. Why this? Because let's face it, the last thing you want is your kid ordering a whole bunch of stuff off of your account because they got ahold of it. We'll go more into family profiles later, but they're something that is certainly worth knowing about, and something to protect.

## Covering your Tracks

If you're a bit creeped out by being tracked all the time, this is something to consider. One thing to remember is the moment that you wake up the device, it'll be listening and recording, and it's not so different from what you track into Chrome, but since it's using your own voice, it might be even creepier. How do you fix this then? Well, you want to go to the settings tab again, choose history, and you can see what Alexa has found you saying, and you can delete all of them. You can go to the device themselves, choosing the one that you want to erase, and then manage the recordings. You should be able to get rid of all of your search history with just the press of a button.

If you haven't rectified these issues already, then now is the time to do so, for the Alexa app is great, and the Alexa system is one of the best, but you must make sure that you add these to your repertoire of information. By doing so, you'll be able to have a much easier and better Alexa experience, and it'll make it better for those that are constantly using this to get something out of it as well.

# 3 Chapter – Using the Amazon Web Services to Create Skills

## The Alexa Service

Are you a bit savvy with computers? Do you have ideas for skills that you would love to put on Alexa devices, but you just don't know how to? Well, there is something that you can now use, and that is the Amazon Web services, and with the Lambda function, you can actually create a whole set of skills. Essentially, it'll run the code only when you need to, and it will scale itself automatically. That means you don't have to run the servers, or any other provisions that are needed. Essentially, it's as simple as uploading the code for the skill into the function, and then lambda will do the rest of it. It's a way to compute resources for yourself.

Now how do you use this? Why do you use this? Well, you're about to find out why many have turned to AWS lambda function to help create skills that you want.

## Why do this?

Now, Alexa has a lot of skills, and the skill kit, along with Amazon web services, allows you to teach Alexa brand new skills. Essentially, it's a new set of abilities that you can enable onto Alexa in order to get questions and requests fulfilled. You can have Alexa look up answers to very specific questions, such as using Google search to give you an answer to something, versus the typical Amazon search engine. It can also be used to help with providing more services to your home, especially controlling devices. Some have even built skills for various games, including tabletop roleplaying games, and that can be used for entertainment. Why would you want this? Well, if you think about it, this basically gives Alexa so much more power, and it does give it the ultimate abilities that it can as a smart assistant.

To begin, you need to choose the skill that you want. They can be one of the following:

- Custom skill: this is used to handle various requests and intents, such as looking up information, playing interactive games, or even ordering from a web service.

- Smart home API: this defines the skills that can help control various home devices, such as your lights, cameras, smart TVs, and even thermostats. It's useful if you have a lot of smart devices.

- Video skills API: this is one that will allow you to handle various video content skills, such as playing movies, shows, changing the channel, and pausing, fast forwarding, or even stopping content.

- Flash briefing: this will give content to the flash briefing.

Most of these skills fall under the first one mentioned, since it's a much larger umbrella.

## What should you Build?

Now, you might have an idea for a skill, but you also need to know where you have to go with it. Different skills that you create do require different types of services. For example, if you're going to make a custom skill, you need to have AWS lambda or a web service. Now, AWS is usually the best one to go for if you've never done this. Why? Well, it lets you run the code on a cloud without having to manage the servers. Essentially, the steps are simple. Alexa will send the requests, you'll inspect the code, take any actions, and then choose the response. If you know Node.js, python, java, or C# then you will be able to write it there. Plus, lots of times with a lot of skills such as putting a Google search engine on your Alexa device, actually have the code already put together, you just need to fix it to make it customizable to your personal account.

Then there is the web service, which is in any cloud hosting service. Essentially, Alexa will send requests to the web service, and the service will take actions to get the response. You can write this in any language, so if you know other computer languages, this definitely might be the best solution.

However, regardless of how you create it, you need to have the custom interaction model for this, which will define the requests that this skill will do, and what users can say in order to get these requests fulfilled.

For example, if you want to control a smart home device, you will need to develop it in AWS lambda. That will take these directives from Alexa and you will have the code to handle this. Then the skill will take the requests usually in the form of the directives to control the device. The code will then handle each of the requests in an appropriate manner. Now, all of the voice interactions that the user has, are done by the Smart Home Skill API, so you don't have to develop it.

If you're doing one with video content, you can use the Video Skill API, and essentially, you'll provide the code, you'll have it receive the directives, handle the requests, and you don't even need to handle the voice interactions.

However, for a flash briefing one, it can be a bit different, since you'll need to create this skill into a developer portal and then configure the RSS or the JSON feeds to monitor the content so that it will be showcased in the following manner. Also as of note, you have to own the content on this too, so definitely keep that in mind.

## Requirements

To create a skill, you do need a few things, and here are what they are, why you need them, and the best way to get them.

The first, is the development portal. No matter what skill you're creating, you got to have this. This is how skills get configured, for this will get information on the skill, including the name, API, the endpoint of this, and other information as well. The Alexa service will use this to help determine the response to requests when the user asks for it.

You also need an internet endpoint for this service, which is essentially AWS lambda, and in this case you need to create an AWS account along with the developer portal account. You can also do an HTTPS web service, but you need a cloud provider and an SSL certificate before you begin.

You need to as well, make sure that you are using the right service for the code that you are going to use. If you're using Java for example, you don't have to go to a third-party service, but instead use AWS. If you don't use one of the major codes, you'll need to have your own web service.

A site to hold any images, files for audio, and video is also good. If you don't need to have these for the skill you're making, then this isn't appropriate for the skill you're developing. If you're stumped on where you can get this, you can get the Amazon simple storage service that AWS offers.

A testing device is another part. That make, it allows you to figure out if the skill works or not, or if it's totally screwed up. You can use a service simulator, but it can be used for device address API or any sort of screen interaction features, so if you're using this with an Echo Show, you won't be able to test that; therefore, it's best to have the device.

**Steps to building this**

It's actually not that hard to build this sort of system. We'll give you the quick and dirty guide to building an AWS skill on lambda.

First, you need to have a voice user interface model. This s what you need before you write any code. This in essence is a flow chart that will show you exactly how a skill will work on the device. You put in the requests that the user will utter, and all of the possible outcomes. This will help to design the various elements of said interface. If you need to add in some other interface elements, such as the Echo Show, you will definitely need to make a chart for that. Typically, the flow diagram will show the skills that will handle, and if there are any images or files, put them on the public site.

Next, set up the skill in the developer portal, where you put the name and invocation name.

Next, take the voice design and use that to build the interaction model. Put the requests in as intents, and you can add slots for various arguments. Sample utterances are examples of what users can say. Dialog model are the various skill requirements that are needed to start Alexa's actions to find the information and respond to the user. You can do this by creating a skill builder, or create an intent schema and sample utterances, and this is typically done in the JSON format.

From this point, you essentially will write and test the code. You should use AWS lambda if you're just beginning with this, and it will allow you to run the code immediately. There are various tutorials that you can use to help you create a skill with a various set of codes, so do look at them to help you build this.

From there, you add in the endpoint of this.

Finally, you can test the skill in the service simulator, or on the Alexa device that you want to try it on, especially if it's an Echo Show device.

Next, you beta test this. Get a small group, have them test it, and have them report the problems. You can then tweak it to fit the model better so that people can actually use this.

Finally, you submit your skill to be certified. It must first pass the submission checklist that is there, and you can look at the requirements for this. You should make sure that it's got everything that you need, and then you can submit it for certification.

After that you can rest easy, or if you really want to, perhaps create another skill to use on your Alexa device.

Creating and enhancing Alexa skills is fun, and this is a tip and trick to giving you a whole smorgasbord of Alexa skills for you to try out on your device. It makes a world of a difference, and it's quite fun too.

## 4 Chapter – Skills Every Alexa Device Should have

With an Alexa device, there are some things that every single one should have. This chapter will go over what they are, a few of the key ones to make sure you've put on your device, and why it is that they should be there.

**Big Sky**

**Big Sky**

Philosophical Creations

★ ★ ★ ✦ ☆  215

ENABLE

Account lin▓▓▓quired

TRY SAYING

"Alexa, open Big Sky."                    "Alexa

ABOUT THIS SKILL

Big Sky: Hyper-local, hourly weather forecasts for Amazon Alexa

Why Big Sky?

If you're looking for a valuable weather app, one of the best ones is Dark sky, and this is a great one that will show you what it's like outside. You might think this is your average weather app, but it's more than that. It shows what it's like directly outside, down the block, and in the neighborhood, and doesn't just give you a general idea of the way it looks outside. Big sky is like Dark Sky, but without the maps, unless of course you're using an Echo Show. It does use the same API, so you'll get the same results; you can just ask Alexa for them if you want an accurate weather reading on what is going on.

## Car help

Have you ever needed an Uber or a Lyft, and you can't seem to find your phone? Or maybe you don't want to peruse through the app? Well, now you can, with the Uber and Lyft skills, you can now get a ride requested without having to pull out the mobile device that you use. It'll tell you how much a ride will cost, and not only that, if you want to see the various cars themselves, you totally can, so long as you have an Echo device that has a screen on it such as the Echo Show.

## Kayak

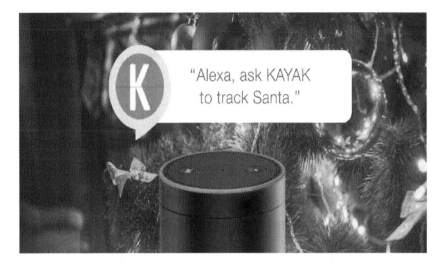

If you're going to go out of town, but you don't really have the time to sit and peruse a ton of websites, why not try Kayak. You need an account for this, but that's simple to create if you don't have one already. From here, you can book hotels of your choosing, get prices for flights, and you can book these flights as well. Another great thing that you can do, is put in your budget, and you can get the recommended trips based on the amount willing to be spent, and also the home airport. It's a great thing to have, especially if you're the type that doesn't want to deal with all the cumbersome bookings and such.

**Fit for life!**

Are you trying to get in shape? Well, that can be quite hard, and it can be quite a struggle to get into the spirit of working out. Luckily, there is an Alexa skill for this, which is called 7-minute workout; it will give you the motivation that you need. You can go through the short workout, and you can take breaks as you need. It only contains one routine, which can get boring after a while, but if you think about it, it's better to have one thing that will get you started than to have nothing at all, and it's a good way to get that beginning motivation to do something further.

## The Magic Door

This is a fun skill that's mostly there to showcase the real depth. It's a fun one that's more for the whole family as an entertainment option, but it's actually one of the best if you want to just go on an adventure that has a lot of fun riddles and activities. It's a great one if you're looking for an entertaining skill that's fun for everyone.

## Jeopardy

If you love the game Jeopardy! This is definitely the skill for you. This is updated each weekday, and it will give you a few clues based on some of the key questions from the show that day. Essentially, you can do this in front of the TV, saying the answers to the questions, and it's a fun game if you want to do something fun with friends, and enhance the competitive spirit.

**Order Pizza**

Ordering pizza has never been easier. With this, you can add the Pizza Hut, and Dominos option in order to determine what types of pizza you want. If you already have an order, you can say that to the device, and Alexa will order this for you. It's a great way to order pizza without having to get up, grab your phone, and navigate. You can do this hands-free, and if you have your information already put in, you can get the results right away.

These are but a few of the many Alexa skills out there for you to choose. If you love to use the Alexa system, then it's time to make sure that you have these skills. They're a ton of fun, and worth all of the time and the effort that you'll put into this, for it's quite fun for everyone to try out, and they're skills that certainly do get a lot of use with each passing day.

# 5 Chapter – How to Set up Profiles

One thing that will immensely help with your Alexa device is set up profiles. You can also set it up with voice recognition if you feel it's needed. It's important to do this if you do have other people in the house that like to use different content, manage features that are appropriate to their account (such as maybe to-do lists, calendars, and even shopping lists). Plus, if you want to create a library for yourself, and for the family, you can do that. Even custom information is important, such as the traffic route for one person to get to where they need to go. Seating up profiles is essential in using this great system. How do you do this though? Well, you're about to find out.

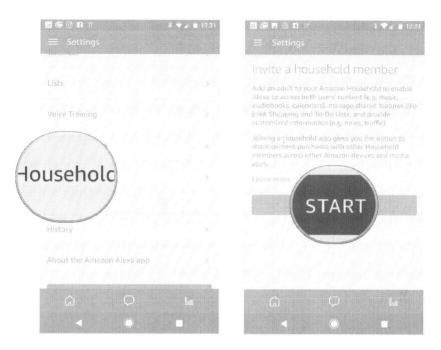

## Adding Users

Now, to add anyone to this, you have to follow just a few tips. You need to have everyone that's in your home present, both adults and children, and then, you can follow the settings needed.

First, you go to settings then accounts, and then choose the tab that says, "household profile." From there, you'll follow the instructions. You'll be asked to put the other people's account information on there, so pass it around so that they can all add to it.

But there are a few things that you will need to keep in mind. When you do have a second adult on there, they can use the cards associated with your account to make purchases. However, you can put a confirmation code there. Another thing that you should watch out is the fact that they can access the Prime photos. However, you can restrict access to the Echo Show.

Another thing to keep in mind is that on the Echo Look, you can only look at and delete the photos on the account, so there is more protection. Alexa will ask which account is the one being used, and then if you do ask to take a photo after switching or after 15 minutes, it will ask for the user.

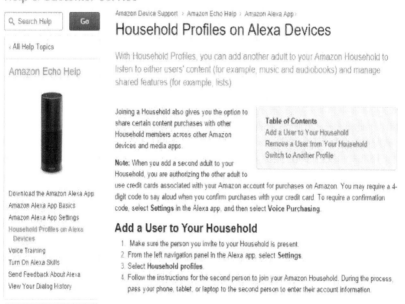

## Switching profiles

One thing that you might want to know more about, is how to switch profiles. Once you set up the household, how you switch accounts is simple. When you want to switch accounts, you can say "Alexa, switch accounts." To verify that you're using the correct account, you can even ask "Alexa, whose account is this?" and you'll get an answer for that. If you're doing it on the app, you use the menu at the top of the screen to toggle between the libraries.

Adults in Jason's Household

Jason Fitzpatrick                               Leave

████ Fitzpatrick                              Remove

## Removing a user

Sometimes, if you're using an Alexa device in a house where someone might want to move out, you'll need to remove their profile. If you do need to remove an adult, you're not able to add it to the same account, or to another account, for about 180 days, so make sure that's what you want to do before you do it. If it's done by accident and you want to re-add it, you can contact customer service. To remove this is simple, and you just have to go to the settings tab in the Alexa app.

From there, you go to accounts once again, and then you can choose "In an Amazon household with (name specified)" and from there, you can choose to remove the user that you want to get rid of. If you're removing yourself, you can choose to leave. It'll prompt you again, so if you for sure want to do this, you can press it again in order to confirm the change that you're making.

Sometimes you need to know how to add and remove profiles from your home. This chapter gave you the know-how on how to do this, and you'd be surprised just how useful this is for yourself, and why you should definitely have this knowledge if you're planning on using this device.

# 6 Chapter – How to Get Alexa to Start Your Day

Did you know that you could use Alexa to kickstart your day? With this, you can pre-program various commands into Alexa to go off at a certain time, or even with a certain command. It's great, but there are a few limits to this. It kicks off at a time or a command that you choose, but in order for this to work, it has to be something that isn't music related, because at this time, you can't include the music player command. However, there are still some great uses for this, allowing you to begin your day, and let's face it, having a routine makes this better.

Now, with the new Echo system, you can enable alarms on it as well, which is super helpful. There are constant updates being made to this, with new features being installed, so it's possible that there will be more additions to this as time goes on.

Right now, you can use news, flash briefing, weather, traffic, or a smart home device. Essentially, it's a way to set up flash briefing to wake up to, and you can add some extra tidbits of information and turn off devices and such, or turn them on when you wake up. It'll get updates though, so hopefully it'll allow music in the future. Currently, if you want to add any feedback, you can go to the help and feedback area of the Alexa app to tell Amazon what they should add. They do listen. They'll work with this.

But, it's not an end-all to the system. In fact, it still allows this to work like a charm, and here is how you use it.

**How to set up Alexa Routines so it's actually useful.**

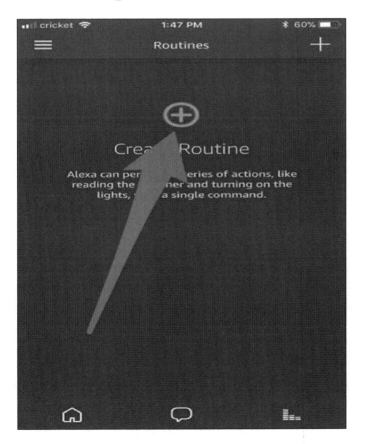

Now, here is how you set it up so that you can get some use out of it. Essentially, you want to go to the main menu of the app, which is that hamburger icon that's located at the top of the screen. It's called that because of the horizontal lines looking almost like a hamburger. Now, you can then when you have the menu open go to a variety of functions, but this time around, we're going to Routines.

Once the Routine option is opened up, you'll see the "start my day" setup as the default option, but of course, this isn't enabled. To enable this, you can tap the icon that's next to it to review it, edit the start time or even the command, and then enable it. To add more routines, you can press the plus icon and then you will set it up as you go along.

Now, once you press the plus button, you will see the routine that's pictured below. Essentially, this is what Alexa will do the second the "trigger" that's stated begins. Currently, there are only two triggers that you can use, the command that you've spoken and specified, or even the scheduled time. If you're the type that wants to say good morning to Alexa before you begin, you'll say "Alexa, good morning" or "Alexa, good night," and that will trigger the command. If you want Alexa to wake you up with a flash briefing, you use the time instead, and that is how it'll wake the system. Now, if you want to, you can press the plus button to change either of these.

Now, the "when this happens" is essentially what will be said to trigger the action. The "Add action" is what action will be done the second either the phrase is uttered or the time. If you want to maybe disable the security system, so long as it's connected to your Alexa system, the add action can be "disable security system" or if you're saying, "Alexa, good night" you can with this action shut down the Alexa system so that it sleeps, and also, turn off all the lights, and even lock your home up. It's pretty weird all that you can do with this.

Now, once you have all of this together, you then will create this.

Now, if you're struggling with what you want the action to be, you'll be given four options to choose from. They are news, traffic, smart home, and weather. There isn't much to be added just yet, but then, you can press one, and then you'll be given various options for each of these routine choices.

Once that's done, you'll be able to then have a routine set up, which is pretty good.

Now, currently it's lacking in some functions, which kind of stinks, and might be a limitation that many aren't into, for the sole reason that they want to have that extra addition. But, considering the fact that the Echo spot is being seen as a bedside alarm clock, it will definitely roll out these additions once it's released.

The Echo spot, in case you don't know, is an Alexa system that essentially looks like an alarm clock, meaning that it will function like one. However, it's got a lot of the Echo Show capabilities to it, which is one of the major benefits of it, since you can have the screen there. It's much smaller, but it does the job well, and it's a good one to have if you're considering getting another Echo device for your room.

This chapter went over the routines option and while it is lacking at this point, it's certainly something to consider if you want to start putting together a better routine using the Alexa system.

## 7 Chapter – Alexa's New Voice Recognition Software

One other feature that's recently made a splash on the Amazon Alexa market, is the fact that Alexa can now recognize voices. Well...sort of Amazon Alexa can to a certain degree, but it's not quite what you're expecting. It is something that can certainly help those that are considering different household profiles, and it's a great function for this. This chapter will discuss what it is, and the importance of it.

**An expanded Tool**

Essentially, when the device owners wanted a way to tell different members apart, the first thing that they wanted was the voice recognition software to tell adults apart from kids. It's something that parents want so that their kids and teens aren't trying to buy stuff, or even access adult rated content.

Alexa does this, but only to a certain degree.

Currently, the only voices that Alexa is able to recognize are those that are adults in the household. Currently, to do this, an Amazon household profile is made for every single adult user, and that's how commands are put in. Currently, the household can have two adults and up to four teens and four children, but as of right now, the Alexa system can only detect up to two adults, so it's important to understand that it does have limitations.

Some might see this as useless, but it's still a very helpful system. Why is that? Well, when you do have this added, adults can still control the purchases, and also accessing adult content.

If you don't want a child to see the adult content, or to restrict their purchasing, the one thing that you will want to do, is to make sure that there is a confirmation pin put in for all of the purchases that are made on the app. If you're setting up profiles, keep this a secret from the other person, and when you do spend money on something, you will then be prompted to ask for the confirmation code and when you do, it'll verify the purchase.

Now, when you do have a second profile on there, it's essentially authorizing the cards to be used with Amazon purchases, which might be a little bit dubious in terms of security, so make sure that you watch out for this as well.

On the Echo Show, it's also of note that you will also have to restrict access on the Prime Photos, so if you don't want the other person to see them, it's restricted in its own way.

## Why Have This Then?

Why have voice recognition then? It doesn't determine the difference between an adult and a child, and you still got to put codes on everything. Well, it allows Alexa to switch to profiles by hearing someone's voice. Now, various profiles can be completely configured in their own way, so if a person wants to merely listen to certain audio books, it'll show up on there. The same goes to streaming music. Whatever profile is active will have everything that is currently on there, just as if it was done manually, so if you want to restrict that content to each profile, it can be done.

For example, if the kids want to listen to some kids' music, you can have their voices be recognized there, and from there, their profile will show up, and that will in turn, play their music, which is pretty nice.

Alexa calls and messaging is affected in this way as well. It would be annoying if you had messages, but had to hear other people's messages, but with the voice profile, you don't need to specifically tell Alexa whose messages needed to be played, or whomever it's from. Once Alexa hears your voice, it will play the messages that you have, and if you want to send something to a contact, it will do so. If you're calling someone else who has an Alexa device, or the Alexa app, it'll tell you which person is calling, and it will soon tell you immediately.

Alexa in this will announce your name to the other Alexa device, so that the other person recognizes that it's you. If you want messages to be played, Alexa will recognize them, and only play the ones that are related to you and your profile. If your partner or another adult decides to use it, it'll play those. The same goes for sending messages. If you have a mutual contact with another user, Alexa will send it with your name attached, since it will in turn recognize your voice.

## How to set this up?

So how do you put it all together? Well, it's actually pretty easy. The first thing you want to do is open up the main menu icon located within the app, which is from the hamburger icon that's at the top of the screen. You then head down to settings and click on that.

You want to from here look at the tab that says, "your voice," click on that, and you'll be taken to a welcome screen that will in turn create a voice profile. You can from here choose the "begin" icon to set this up. If you change your mind and for some reason want to do this later, then you can press the option that says so.

You'll then be given a screen that urges you to teach Alexa your voice. You want to first select the device that you are nearby to speak to. If you only have one Echo device, then you'll just press that one. From there, you will then press the next button, and you'll be prompted with 10 phrases that Alexa will want you to say. You say them, and then Alexa will analyze your voice and create a voice recognition system that sets that profile as yours. It's that simple.

Once that's finished, you can then let the other adult in the household repeat these steps with their own Alexa profile. You can learn about switching profiles in an earlier chapter as well to help with this.

That's all you need to do to set this up, and that's really how it can be used. Now, if you want to include it to recognize various children in the household for extra security, Amazon might start to expand on this if enough people do ask for it. It can be done with the feedback form in the Alexa app. Currently, it's available on the site, and on the app as well, which is definitely something to consider if you want to add this feature.

Voice recognition is very important, and this chapter highlighted how to enable this with the Alexa system, so that you're able to achieve the best results possible, and the right recognition needed for your profiles.

# 8 Chapter – Alexa and Cooking

Do you know how useful Alexa is with cooking? Well, you're about to find out. We touched a little bit on this with the Allrecipes and the Food Network system, but, we're going to go into more details on how Alexa can help in the kitchen, in order to make you a killer chef that can make anything you want.

## Best Recipes

Now, let's say that you want to cook something, but you're limited on ingredients, and the last thing you want to do is go to the store. Best Recipes is by Hellman's and it allows you to take ingredients that you have in order to create recipes that are totally possible. This works with both lunch, dinner, and even breakfast recipes. Now, it will email the skills, but you can ask for visuals as well if desired.

## Food Network

This is in the same vein as Allrecipes, but it takes it a step further. This is probably the ideal in kitchen visuals, since it takes the Echo Show's ability to showcase a recipe and will do so on the screen itself.

You can look at photos and the ingredients that are listed, but it also will give you actual videos of the recipe that you're creating, so you can get an idea of what you're making. This will allow you to pinpoint if you screwed something up, rectify it, and from there, create more delicious content. This is probably the future of cooking, and it does work wonders.

## Substituting Ingredients

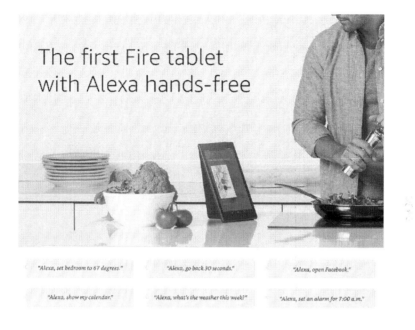

The first Fire tablet
with Alexa hands-free

"Alexa, set bedroom to 67 degrees."     "Alexa, go back 30 seconds."     "Alexa, open Facebook."

"Alexa, show my calendar."     "Alexa, what's the weather this week?"     "Alexa, set an alarm for 7:00 a.m."

Do you want to change a recipe because the ingredients aren't per your diet? Or maybe you want to cook something, but you don't have the ingredient on hand? Well, you don't have to worry about that problem, because Ingredient Sub is an Alexa cooking skill that will allow you to substitute items. It has a lot of basics on there, so it might not be fitting for complex diets, but if you're looking for healthy alternatives, this is certainly the place to go.

## Cooking food Safely

The last thing anyone wants to have is to either serve overcooked or undercooked food. It's either embarrassing, or generally unhealthy. However, by downloading the Cook reference skill, it will tell you the safest temperature to cook everything, which will save you a Google search. It has most of the common meats on there, so you don't have to go too far in order to find this information, and it does work wonders for you.

## Grocery Shopping Made Easy

"Alexa, order a picnic basket."

Now, if you want to add items to the grocery list, but you don't feel like jotting it down constantly with a pad and a pen, you can use the Chefling skill in order to keep track of what you need to buy. But that's not all, it will allow you to know when food is about to expire, and by simply opening up the app, Alexa will do the rest of the work. You can add various items to the list, share shopping lists with others, and also check and verify expiration dates to keep your kitchen the best it can be.

**Grilling King**

If you've wanted to grill, but you've struggled with it, there is a skill called Grilling Time and Heat Master, which will allow you exactly how long you need to grill something, based on the meat, veggie, or fish that you're throwing on there. It'll also tell you what temperature is best, whether it should be done directly or indirectly, and even how long you should keep it there. If you've ever wanted to get good at grilling, this is the way to go, and it's so simple that practically anyone can do it themselves.

**Storing Fruits and Veggies Right**

The one thing that stinks is when you buy some fresh fruit or produce, and then you need up not using it, causing it to expire. You might end up putting it somewhere, forgetting about it, and then it's too late to use it. The Fruit Stand skill will tell you the best place to store a fruit or veggie, and where it should go to live the longest. Of course, it can also tell you the average shelf life too, so that you can throw it somewhere so that you don't forget it.

## Spice Master

Herbspice is a skill that will allow you to become the master of herbs and spices that you should be. To be honest, lots of people don't know how to use herbs and spices effectively, and a lot don't even know of some that exist. But, this skill will allow you to get random facts about the roots, plants, and the seeds, which in turn will make you a better cook. You can even use this in herbal medicine, such as in the case of you're feeling nauseous. You can then take some ginger and it's a naturally way to stay healthy. You can also learn how to use these herbs in the kitchen for best results too.

## Get Seasonal Foods

Finally, you can find out what's in season, which in turn will allow you to get various fruits and veggies into your diet in order to be healthier. You can get the Farmer's Market skill, and this will tell you what's in season around you, and you can from there go to your local farmer's market and pick up what they have to offer. Eating local and home grown will allow you to get the full benefits of these natural foods, and this skill will in turn allow you to do just that as well.

When it comes to cooking, Alexa can help you a lot, and with the skills and various helpful tidbits listed here, you can use Alexa to your advantage in order to have the best cooking skills that you can have. Gone are the days where you're fumbling in the kitchen for a recipe, for Alexa and the Echo Show can work in tandem to give you everything that you need to be the best chef you can be.

# 9 Chapter – Alex and Baby care (New Features to Help Parents)

If you're a new parent, you might wonder how the Echo Show can help with this. Well, you're about to find out, for here are some of the best Alexa skills to help expecting parents and parents that have already had a child take care of it in an even better manner.

## Drop-In

Drop-in can be used as a baby monitor. That's actually one of the best ways to check on your baby. By simply asking Alexa to do this, it will give you live feed from another Echo system, which you can put in the child's room. This will allow you to check on them, and saves money on baby monitors.

Now, it's important that for this to work, you need another Echo device, so get an Echo dot for this. It's also good to use with older kids as well to make sure that they're doing okay.

**Hatch Baby**

This is a smart nursery app, here prints can ask the doctor various recommended information, such as various diaper changes, how many they need, the weight of the child, when it was fed, and also how much sleep it got. You can ask Alexa how many dirty diapers the child has had, how long the child has slept, and also can record the diaper changes as well.

Now, you can use this on its own, but if you have a smart changing pad, or a hatch baby grow system, you'll be able to track this even more, including weight, and feeding amounts. The changing bed has a connected scale, which you can get insight on the development of the baby, and get doctor information in order to ensure that the child is taken care of.

## Baby Stats

This will let you track the diapers both wet and stool, weight, feedings, when you've pumped, and also the baby's sleep. You don't have to track everything, just what you want to track. You simply ask "Alexa, ask the baby to add (stat you want to add) and from there it'll be added. It's best to have this along with the mobile app to track all of this correctly. You can ask Alexa to get the baby's stats as well, in order to make sure proper growth and wellness is maintained.

It's a newer Alexa skill, but if you want to check to make sure that you're feeding the kid enough, and doing enough for them, this is the way to go.

## What to Expect

This is perfect for expectant mothers. To use this, you need to enable the skill, put in your information about your pregnancy, and from there, get tracking's immediately on whatever is going on in order to have a pregnancy that is both happy and healthy. If you need to, you can also adjust these dates as well, especially if you find out that your child is coming earlier. You also can use this after the baby is born too, up to the first year in order to make sure that the child is in optimal health. This is a great one to just track everything, and for those that want to make sure their fertility is in check, this can be a great skill to help, and one that can get you started on a great path. It's free too.

**BabyCenter**

BabyCenter also has the same sort of skill similar to What to Expect. This one as well will give you stats on the baby, what you should do next as a parent, and the like. It's important to consider using this one as well, because it is one of the first skills in this category, and it helped to pioneer the way to making sure that you get the most out of your child's health. It is good for both expecting parents to watch their pregnancy, and also for babies as soon as they are born to make sure that they're healthy.

It can be hard for expecting parents to get the job done. It's not easy to raise a child, but with the Echo Show and Alexa, you can have the visual system that you need, along with Alexa there to record information and tell you this. By using this, it can help you track the pregnancy more and more, which in turn will make it more worthwhile for everyone, and it will allow you to have a happy and healthy baby right there, with the help of the Alexa system.

## 10 Chapter – Locks and Security

There is a certain peace of mind that comes with being able to check on or set your security system with your voice or remotely, but there are also associated security concerns, more so than with integration of other appliances. Because of this, your options are somewhat more limited when it comes to alarms, locks, and other security measures than they are with lights or temperature control.

Until recently, integrating Alexa with a security system meant buying one of the security system hubs mentioned in Chapter 2. Even then, these systems don't offer things like smart lock integration. Many people are understandably dubious about putting voice control technology into their front door; it is only recently that technology has advanced to the point these items offer more convenience than risk.

## Scout Alarms

The only pure security system that integrates directly with Alexa is the Scout Alarm system. Costing around $300, the Scout Alarm system is a wireless home security system that comes in two colors (Arctic or Midnight) and offers customizable self-installation, without any wiring or drilling. Scout's monitoring is available with a month-by-month contract, as well, which means you don't have to lock yourself into a long-term contract when you're first testing the system out.

The Scout system offers a wide array of Alexa commands to give you the maximum in home security without a lot of hassle. You can customize the notifications you receive to be as comprehensive (or not) as your lifestyle requires. With the Alexa control, your Scout system lets you set or check on your security system remotely, with a live activity feed on your smart phone and various alerts that can be set through the accompanying app.

## Smart locks

A smart lock is just what it sounds like: a standard door lock that also is compatible with smart phone apps to give you a wider range of control and information, both when you're at home and when you're using it remotely. Smart locks are not a new concept, and you'll find several on the market, but the ability to use voice control with them through Alexa is a relatively recent develop.

As of this writing, the only smart lock that integrates fully with Alexa is the **August Second Gen Smart Lock**. Even here you can't lock or unlock your door with voice commands, but Alexa will tell you the status of the lock, giving you some peace of mind when you're not able to physically check on the lock's status. This August model costs around $200 and does require professional installation.

Smart locks have some unique abilities that you might not think about right off the bat. Most of them can sense your presence through your smart phone and automatically unlock when you get home, a big help if you're coming back from a shopping trip or otherwise have your hands full. You can also issue temporary digital keys to other smart phones, granting short-term access to babysitters, contractors, or house-sitters without having to worry about making (and then collecting) extra physical keys.

## Alexa security concerns

When it comes to your home's security, Alexa as a service can enhance your home's capabilities, but it also does come with its own concerns. The primary security concern that most people raise when discussing smart home technology is the extent to which Alexa listens on and records your day-today life.

Alexa only actively listens to what you're doing in your house after you say the wake word, but it does have the potential to listen in any time the microphones are activated. Some people have raised concerns about the fact that Alexa could be hacked to tell potential criminals who is home and when by listening to their voice patterns and footsteps. Concerns have also been raised about Alexa recording all the interactions you have with it, opening the door for potential identity theft.

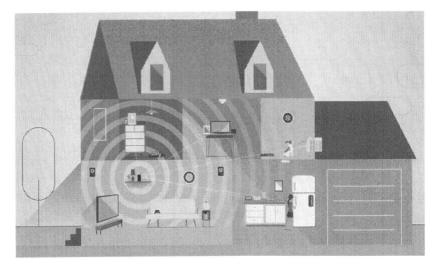

To this second point, you can delete the recorded interactions from the Cloud if you so choose, or even set Alexa to not make these recordings in the first place. This will inhibit the program's ability to learn your preferences and voice patterns; it's up to each user exactly what level of recording they're comfortable with.

To the first point, you can also use the "mute" function on your Echo to turn off the microphones whenever you want. Muting your Echo completely deactivates the vocal processor, meaning it must be activated and deactivated manually by pressing a button, but if you're concerned about people listening in uninvited, muting your Echo when it's not in use can give you some extra peace of mind.

It should be noted that, as of yet, there have been no documented incidents of people using the voice commands of Alexa to gain unauthorized access to a user's home systems. Even the potential concerns about smart locks are at this point mainly hypothetical, and the security will only tighten as these products are further developed.

# 11 Chapter – How to Get Alexa to Play Music, movies, and videos

Alexa has the ability to play music, movies and videos with this amazing system. With the Echo Show, it changes this as well. Here is how you can reap the benefits of this, and get Alexa to do all of this for you easily.

## Music

When it comes to music, Alexa has you covered. Not only

that, you can now look at the lyrics on various songs if you want to see them through the Echo Show. But how do you play music? Well, here is how.

If you have a personal playlist from either iTunes, Google Play, or other various means, you go to "My Music" on the Amazon site via the computer. Put the music there, and once it's all up there, you can ask Alexa to play this by saying the name of the song, and it'll play it. You can do up to 250 songs with My Music, and that's free. But if you want to upload more, you need to get an Amazon music Storage subscription, and from there, you can play any music that you want. However, if you buy something from the digital music store or autorip eligible CDs/records don't actually count towards the limit, so keep that in mind.

You can also play it on Bluetooth. To do this, you need to make sure that you have a Bluetooth connection, and from there, you can simply choose the song, or have Alexa do so. You need to make sure these are synched up though.

To play this on multiple Echo devices, such as maybe through the house, you can go to the smart home tab, then choose groups, create group, multi room music, and from there, you can then choose the Echo devices for this, and you can custom name this too. Once you've decided it, you can create groups and that'll make those Echo devices a group. Once you do that, you can have Alexa turn these on, and then have Alexa play music, and you can control the volume of this by saying "set volume for group to level X" and it'll automatically do that. You can't do Bluetooth connected speakers currently however, so keep that in mind.

With the ability to stream all sorts of audio, the Amazon Echo can read the news to you, stream your favorite local radio stations and play various forms of audio, such as podcasts and more from Amazon's own multimedia offerings. The Amazon Echo offers tremendous built-in streaming options, however, if the available options do not meet your needs, there is always the option to use the Echo as a Bluetooth speaker and stream virtually anything you want. Let's say your favorite podcast isn't available through Spotify, or you want to watch a movie from your laptop but want to amp up the volume; just circumvent the Amazon Echo's official support and you can stream practically any audio through the Echo using Bluetooth.

Media streaming services that Alexa supports currently are your own Amazon Music Library, as well as Amazon Prime music, Spotify, Pandora, iHeartRadio, TuneIn, Audible, and some of the ebooks from your Kindle library. Streaming Apple music from your iPhone or Google Play music from your Android requires pairing your device with the Amazon Echo using Bluetooth and selecting it as the audio output.

Even a connection via Bluetooth allows you to control the

audio that's playing through voice recognition. For instance, you can say "Alexa, pause" and whatever audio is playing will pause. Or say "Alexa, next" and whatever audio is playing will move to the next audio item.

Some people believe that they don't have time, or that listening to podcasts is a hassle. Mostly this belief comes from those who are only familiar with the ones that you have to actually sit down and register for. Sure there are a lot of those premium-fee based podcasts out there and those you must have a subscription to listen to. However, there are also lots of totally free podcasts out there that do not require a registration. It's true that the free podcasts are fueled by ads and marketing, however most podcasters have learned to keep those ads as short as possible to keep the listeners' attention. There are also super short podcasts, sometimes only fifteen minutes long, that typically have no ads at all. TuneIn is a good site that streams a few good free podcasts. TuneIn has been mentioned earlier in this guide as one of those third-party apps that can be integrated with Alexa. To find podcasts that interest you, go to the TuneIn site and use the search box to search for a podcast topic that may interest you. You can also check out TuneIn's Top podcast page for those that may be of some value to you personally.

Please bear in mind that some of these podcasts can be broadcast from all around the world. Any one of those services can experience difficulties, such as servers and networks being down, episodes posted late, etc. There could be occasions where you say "Alexa, play (podcast name)," and she replies back, "Sorry, I can't play (podcast name) now." It most likely won't happen often, but don't be surprised when you hear this type of response from Alexa on occasion.

Much like how music files owned by the user can only be played from the Amazon Music Library, audiobooks that the user owns can only be played from the Echo's Audible Library. You can play your audiobooks through your Amazon Echo using an audiobook service called Audible, and control them using your voice. If you have a particular Kindle book you'd like Echo to play, and the particular book supports the Echo device, you will most likely notice a difference in the voice of Alexa, as it will sound slightly more robotic than other audiobooks you've listened to.

It's super easy to set up your Audible account and use your Echo to read your audiobooks. Since Amazon owns Audible and the two are tightly integrated, as long as you are logged into your Amazon account on your Echo, Audible is always ready to go. Make sure you have an Audible subscription to get started listening to audiobooks whenever you are ready.

## How to Play Movies on the Echo Show

The Echo Show can play movies if you so desire. If you want to watch something, you first need to enable the skills that are available that allow you to watch something, such as HBO, Showtime, and Starz. With all of these, you will need a subscription, so make sure that you have that.

Now, to watch this, you simply ask Amazon to show you the titles based on the title itself, the genre, the actors, or other factors. You can then say, "Alexa play ____" and it will do that. You can use your voice to control the playback as well.

If you for example have a Netflix account and you want to watch the next episode of "Orange is the New Black" you simply tell Alexa "Play Orange is the New Black, Season 1 Episode 2" and it'll do that.

For Amazon video, you get this automatically with a prime subscription, and you need to make sure that your Echo Show is linked to wherever your Fire TV or other device is. You can also watch this on the Echo Show by saying "on Echo Show" if you don't have one, or if you don't want to watch it on the Fire TV. You can simply go through the library, ask Alexa "show me my video library" if you don't know what to watch, find specific titles that work for you, and look at various media based on certain actors. With all of this, you have control, and Alexa can help you out.

## Watching Videos

You can watch YouTube right from the comfort of your Echo Show? How do you do that? Well, here is how.

First, you need to make sure that YouTube is enabled on this. Obviously go to the app, choose the skill, and enable it. simple as that. From there, you can say "Alexa play YouTube music" and you can from there have Alexa play various videos. You can ask for Alexa to give you video suggestions too, especially if you want to watch a video about cats, dogs, whatever it is that you want. You will then immediately be able to play what you want to watch. The cool part is, you don't even have to touch the system. Alexa will play it for you. You can then listen and enjoy whatever it is that you want to on the Echo Show.

The Echo Show is a great device for those that love to play media. You can even connect this to the Fire TV if you want to stream it, but make sure that if you do this specify whether you want it to be on the Echo Show or Fire TV, because that is definitely something to consider.

Amazon and the Echo Show are working together to give you media that you can control with your voice. It's amazing all that you can do with it, and almost magical if you think about it. You have the control directly at your disposal, and it's something that you can take full advantage of and learn for yourself, in order to get the most out of this smart device.

# 12 Chapter – Installing classic Radio on Alexa

With Alexa, there are so many different skills out there for you to choose. However, some of us like the classics and having those recordings bring your imagination to life. Classic radio is something that's originally from the golden age of Hollywood, and for many young people in this day and age, it is often met with a questioning look, since most people don't even listen to that. It's a fun form of entertainment, and it's something that with Alexa, you can get once more, and without too many hoops to jump through.

Well, the nice thing about Alexa is that not only Alexa can read books to you from the audible library, but there is another skill that you can enable to enjoy this sort of experience. There is a group called the Old Time Radio Researchers Group Library that has uploaded thousands of those classic old time radio shows that you can download and stream for free. That's right, you don't have to pay a thing if you have it downloaded.

Now, why would you at this? Well, if you're someone that enjoys classic radio, it's a great way to push those old recordings back into ears of modern people. They're often seen as something that only a few people know about, but they're very fun, and there can even be entertaining stories for children. The library that put this together is a nonprofit, so all of these are public domain and it's not for profit. That's why it can be legally downloaded and played on your Alexa device. You can donate if you want to, and you don't need to register or anything else. It's a great system, and definitely one of those Alexa skills that most people don't discuss.

**How to put this on there**

There are a few steps to put these on there, and here is how you do it.

First, you go to the home page and look at the guidelines and rules. Make sure to read them. From there, go to the alphabet links that are located on the left side and search it by letter. You can then click on the title of what you want to listen to and the episodes.

Now, if the titles are links, you'll need to download them. You can also go "save link as" and then it'll download as mp3. Now, depending on the browser, it might ask you to also save it. You'll get a direct link to this, and it won't take you to a separate page.

Now as of note, some of these shows have a different detail page, and you might see that links are shown in the upper part and the more information is in the lower part. If you click the links at the top, you'll stream the episodes. You'll want to download them to play on your device.

Now, if you press the blue icon to download, it will stream it automatically, but if you right click it, that's where you'll get the option to download. If you want to download every episode in a single torrent file, you can do it as well.

Now, you put these straight onto your Echo or whatever Alexa device that you have. You can even put them on your Echo Show as well. To do this, you put the files onto the Amazon music library, make sure to edit the tracks so that when you ask Alexa for them you're not barking out a ton of numbers, and from there, you simply ask Alexa to play them for you in the same way you would any other track that you have in the library. It's that simple, and it's cool.

You can also do it in another way. You can connect the computer where the files are to your Echo device via Bluetooth. In this case, directly use the music or media player that the computer already has to play them. You won't be able to tell Alexa to navigate, so keep that in mind, because that's often something that is a big deal if you're going for the full hands-free experience.

Now if you're a fan of any of this, this could be the perfect thing for you. It might seem weird right now, but it's actually a classic form of music listening that many people tend to enjoy. If you're a fan of the golden age, some of the old radio shows that used some fun and amazing sound effects to get the point across, then this is for you. Now that it's available to play on your Echo device, it can actually change the whole thing for you, and it's a lot of fun to learn about as well.

# 13 Chapter – Controlling Smart home devices with Alexa

Alexa and the Echo Show can control smart home devices. How does it do it through? Well, you're about to find out.

To begin, you first need an Echo Show that is connected with the Alexa app. If you don't have that already, get one, download the app, and sync these together. Also, keep in mind the place where you've put your Echo Show. It might not seem like much, but one thing that you need to consider is that it will be controlling all of the smart home devices, so make sure that it's in an area with a strong Wi-Fi signal, and if it's not, you should definitely consider moving this. If your house is too big for Alexa to register some smart home devices, pick up another Echo dot for some extra help.

From here, it's time to set up the smart home devices. You need to get some first, and for the setup of this, you typically do it just like normal. You're going to give this a name though, so make sure that you give it something that you're okay with calling it, and something that is clear, concise, and able to be understood easily. Things such as "kitchen light" or "living room lamp" work great.

Once this is done, you need to introduce Alexa to them and get it to recognize them as well. Typically, you can say "Alexa, discover new devices" and after a few seconds, it'll scan the area and add gadgets that are found, and you'll be able to control them after.

If you don't have the ability to do so, you'll have to manually set it up yourself. You'll need to go to the smart home section, go to "smart home skills" and from this point forward you should search for the skills that you want to enable. Nest and Lutron for example require you to do this, and you need to login in order for Alexa to take control of this. You need to authorize this since it does involve cameras and such.

Next, you need to group everything. If you're wanting Alexa to control more than one similar device, you should group these together. There are also other groups called scenes.

Groups are what they literally are, which are devices that are behind one single name, such as the kitchen lights working together. Instead of asking Alexa to turn on one by one, you can group these together. To make this, you go to the Alexa app, click on the smart home section, go to Groups, and then Create Group. Give it a specific name for it to be recognized with and then choose the devices you want to include.

Scenes are when you put some multiple devices in to certain

settings. You don't create them with the Alexa app though, and instead you import scenes from the direct devices, and you can create an IFTT recipe in certain cases as well to make this.

For example, if at night you want the bulbs to be a certain brightness setting, you can make a scene with these lights and such. When you look to discover this, it'll find the scene, and you can ask for it to be activated. It's that simple.

## All About IFTT

IFTTT is a specialized way to connect the hardware and services. Now, if you want to automatically have something happen when a condition is met, such as the front porch lights come on when it's dark out, you can create an IFTT recipe to help make this possible. You need to download the IFTT app and create a login for this before you begin. You can then create recipes, choose the devices that are connected to it, and then automatically generate a new recipe that can be used to help with improving your smart home.

It's still a newer system, and it's getting the kinks still fixed in them, but it's definitely something that you should consider. It will bring the dream of having a smart home that is futuristic and new to the forefront, and it definitely does help if you want to control your smart home devices all at once. Plus, this can be used not just for smart home devices, but also for personal elements of your life, such as if you miss a message, Alexa automatically notifies you on ToDo List or something like that.

With Alexa, you can control your smart home with just your voice. It's bringing homes and other devices to the future, and for those of us that want to make a huge difference in the life of our smart home, this is the way to do it, for it can totally change the way you control things, and your life as well.

# 14 Chapter – The Drop In Function and How to Use It

The Drop In function is something that is useful to many, but often gets criticized back of the lack of privacy that this gives to people. But, if you bought an Echo Show, it's important to realize that you have this system, and it's a valuable function that can certainly help you. so, what in the world is it? Why does it matter? Well, you're about to find out, and you'll learn why some people love, yet also dislike this interesting system.

## What is it?

Have you ever seen those intercom systems that others have had installed in their homes, where they will press a button to check in on someone? That's essentially what this is. Drop In is a means to let users listen to the speakers on a device from one Echo Show to another, or from the smartphone app. It allows one to check in on others, or to call someone if they need to get clarification on something.

Think about it. This could be useful for those that are cooking dinner and want to let their kids know. It's a means to call others, and let them know about the state of something. It's an interesting functionality that does allow one to instantly connect to other Echo devices without using your hands, and it will allow you to check on other Echo devices not in the home as well. Obviously, it's best that you do realize the privacy nature of this, so you need to make sure that you grant permission to this, so make sure that you're okay with this. You will have to enable it yourself, so you won't accidentally do it, which is pretty neat.

## How to use It

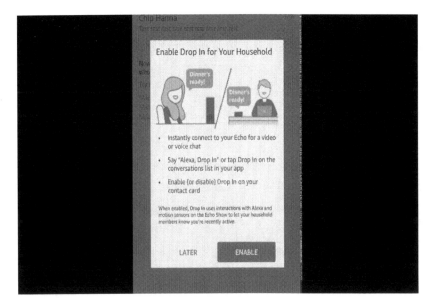

How you use it is simple. First, you need an Echo system to Drop In on, and one to start the drop in. For starting the drop in, you can use the Alexa app as well. You need to make sure that you sign up for Alexa calling and messaging, which will allow it to call and message others. It will then allow you to enable Drop In on who you want to Drop In on, such as maybe an Echo device in the playroom or something. You can then have a contact use Drop In on you if you so desire, but that is optional.

You can then say "Alexa, Drop In on ____" whether it be the name of the Echo device or the name of a contact, and Alexa will allow you to speak to the other Echo. When you do get a Drop In on the device that you have, you'll see a green and pulsing light, and you can then connect and heat everything within range. If you're using the Echo Show and so is the other, you will then be given an option to video chat. You can turn that off though if you don't want to, either by selecting it, or saying "video off" and it won't chat with you. You can also put in Do Not Disturb to block any drops on a specific device for a temporary amount of time, so keep that in mind.

If you want to have a great intercom system though that works wonders and can help, this is the way to do it. It's the future, and you can use this in a variety of ways. Try it out, see if you like it, and try to use Alexa to Drop In on others. It's a bit of a different system, but it can bring everything to the future for yourself, and it definitely is worth it. ☐

# 15 Chapter – Useful Tips and Tricks

Now that you know about the Echo Show, it's time to take a bit of time to customize this for you. Here are a few things to allow you to get the most out of this device.

## Customize your Drop In Function

If you haven't already, customize who drops in on you. If you don't want people dropping in and trying to start audio or video calls, you can customize this by going to the Alexa app, going to the Echo Show device, choosing to drop in, and press "only in my household" which will prevent outside people from dropping in. When you turn it back on, you will need to approve which ones can drop in, so go to the Conversations part of the app, choose the contact, and then press "Contact can Drop In Anytime" to enable this.

## Setting Up Do Not Disturb

If you're overwhelmed by people messaging you or contacting you, you can enable Do Not Disturb. You first swipe down the screen at the top of the app. You should look for the on-demand button that you see to turn on the DND function, and from there, you won't receive anything, whether it be calls, messages, or other notifications. You can schedule it as well.

From the Echo Show's menu, go to Settings, move down to Do Not Disturb and select that to set up a schedule.

## Creating a Background Photo

If you're someone that doesn't like the standard background, you can upload a photo to the background from the app itself.

To do this, go to settings move down, and press the button that is in blue called Choose a Photo and from there you can choose a photo, crop it as needed, and then put it up. You'll immediately see this directly on the Echo Show, which is Neat

## Adjusting the Sound

If you're a bit annoyed by the sounds that you hear, there are a few ways to adjust this. You should, from the Echo Show itself, choose the settings tab and go down to sounds. You can choose the alarm, notification, and also any sounds that you need, such as reminders. You can also turn it off if you don't want to hear any period, which is nice.

## Talking Rather than Touching

If you're a bit weirded out by talking to the device, don't sweat it. However, if you want to make your life easier, you should make sure that you do try to work on using your voice for it. You don't have to, but it's nice.

You can also give Alexa commands, and if you want to opt in for touch, you can as well.

There are two ways to open up virtually anything on the Echo Show. They're either touching, or talking. You can choose either or. Talking is often a bit easier for some people, but if it still weirds you out to talk to the device, or maybe you're getting used to using it, try maybe touching the device rather than talking.

**Say Cheese!**

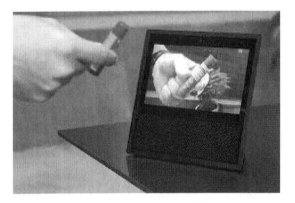

Another great function of the Echo Show is that you can take pictures with it, which is totally different from the other Echo devices. To do this, you can open up the camera app or tell Alexa "Alexa, open the camera" and it will then give you three camera options for you to try out. You can choose one, tell Alexa the number that you want, and Alexa will take a picture. You don't even have to use your fingers, you can actually have Alexa do it all for you. It's a way to totally automate all of this, and it can change the way pictures are taken.

## Going home

If you're sick of having to scroll through menu after menu to go back to the home screen, fear not. Alexa can take you directly back to the home menu, and it doesn't take all that much work. Obviously, you can swipe the screen from the top of the display and press the home button, but wouldn't you like this to be easier? If you say, "Alexa go home" you'll get Alexa to take you back to the home screen, which is also kind of humorous as well.

## A Digital Photo Frame

Building on what you could do before, you can actually turn the Echo Show into a photo frame. If you want to take a photo that you took with someone you love as the Echo Show background, or even have the Echo Show showcase this picture, what you do is go to Prime Photos, and from there select the album that you want to put on there. That's right, just upload the picture of pictures to there, and then ask Alexa to show this off. Simply say "Alexa, show my ____ album" and the blank is whatever you named it. You can make this a slideshow, or even a singular show, whatever it is that you desire.

The Echo Show is a newer device, but that doesn't mean it doesn't already have its own unique tips and tricks. This chapter gave you the information that you need in order to get the most out of your Echo Show. Start to use this today, and work on getting the most out of this. Your Echo Show is a valuable device, and you'll realize, as you continue to play around with it, that there are so many options and functions you have yet to discover.

## 16 Chapter – Managing data Usage with Your Device

One huge part of the Alexa system that lots of people forget about, is data. Of course, they don't really realize that it's a problem until they get their internet bill the next month, but data usage is something that should always be considered when you're looking at an Alexa device. This chapter will discuss some of the factors that you need to keep in mind if you're going to use the Alexa system, and what are some of the ways to manage the data usage on your device.

## How Much data does it use?

You might wonder how much data Alexa uses. It really all depends on what you're doing with it. When you play a song from Amazon Music directly, it actually is directly downloaded rather than streaming. There are two that are downloaded at once, and naturally, that isn't too big of an issue.

Now, if you're doing music from a streaming service, you actually will be using way more data, and that's what's going to end up getting you. If you're someone that isn't changing your mind a lot, you're not going to be using data either, but if you're changing your mind a whole lot, running a ton of apps, demanding Alexa to do everything and not giving it a break, well, guess what? You're going to be using a lot more data. It really all depends on what you're doing with it.

Another big part of it, is how much you leave it on. If you leave the Alexa device on for a long time, demanding it to stream music, play movies, or whatever, it can end up costing you a lot of data, and that can be a problem later on. It's really all dependent on what you're doing with it, and what sorts of actions you're trying to accomplish with this.

Now as well, with some of the other apps that are being put forward, especially shopping, it can definitely start to eat data. This is sometimes a consideration, especially if you're using an internet plan that only has a certain amount of data, and let's face it, everyone hates data caps, but if you're considering bringing Alexa on the go, this can be a huge problem.

If you're tethering your phone to either an Echo dot, or an Echo tap, or if you're tethering an Alexa device to your cell phone for whatever reason, this is a way to create problems for yourself, and your device. If you have an unlimited data plan though, it won't be a huge problem, because if you've got enough data, you don't have to worry. But, if you're not someone that's got an unlimited data plan, then you should definitely consider where your data is going, and in the next section, we'll highlight everything that gets downloaded, and what you'll want to consider if you're trying to save data.

You definitely don't know this until it's too late, or if you get educated on it right away. By understanding how to use this information, you'll save yourself a ton of headaches, and prevent yourself from being totally screwed over by overusing data.

## Data interactions

Now, various interactions do take up a certain amount of data, and really, your best bet is to be wary about when the system is on, when you're streaming, and if you're using your cell phone data service, or if it's hooked to the WIFI in the home.

Now, if you ask Alexa to tell you a joke, convert measurements and currency, or other small little quips, chances are you're not using any data at all, and it takes a whole lot of effort in order to use up a ton of data in this fashion. I mean, it's totally possible to ruin your data cap, but you'd have to be asking Alexa questions constantly to be affecting that.

It's the streaming that will get you. If you use the Amazon music and video service to stream, use Audible, or any other site that requires you to stream, such as Pandora or Spotify, then chances are, you're going to use a lot of data. With Amazon, you'll always be getting a certain amount of audio downloaded, and these files might be kind of big. That's because it will prevent any connectivity issues. If you think about it, it's similar to DVR where it's always recording up to an hour so that you'll be able to rewind to the part that you want to see, or fast-forward to that location. It's important to note that if you are streaming at any time, it's going to download a larger file, which in turn will affect your data, and the overall limit to this.

Now, when you use Amazon Music or video, it'll download the file that you've requested along with the next one. For example, if you have a workout playlist and you tell Alexa to play a certain song, chances are that the second file is also downloaded as well. Many times, people don't even realize that it happens, but it's almost like a surreptitious thing done to keep the state of the system at the top shape it can be. It's to enhance overall performance, and while the intentions are good at the bottom of it all, if you don't know this, it could totally kill your data.

Now, how much data does that take? Well, it's about 5 MB for each song that's of average length, about five or so minutes. Once the first is over, the third song will be added to the queue, and then the second one will be played.

Now, if you're someone who loves to skip music around, this is where you're going to get burned. If you jump from playlist to playlist, you're going to be downloading so many songs. Now if you listen to all of them, great, but chances are you aren't going to be, and if you do skip the tracks, you're going to eat through your data super quickly. This is the same with videos, since often, it's done in tracks or chapters, such as in the case of movies. Let's say you're watching chapter 1, then chapter 2 is downloaded too. But then, if you jump from chapter 1 to chapter 3, or episode 1 to episode 3, you're going to end up killing your data. It's important to be considerate of this, since often, if you're not, this is a huge part of why some struggle with the Alexa system.

Burning through data is something that many people don't even realize that they do until it's too late. But it's imperative to learn this, to get a better feel for it, and to understand it, and this chapter will give you everything that you need to know about data usage. It's a tip that's often not discussed, so you should definitely consider this one, since it could save your data in the long run.

# 17 Chapter – How to Set up Profiles

One thing that will immensely help with your Alexa device is set up profiles. You can also set it up with voice recognition if you feel it's needed. It's important to do this if you do have other people in the house that like to use different content, manage features that are appropriate to their account (such as maybe to-do lists, calendars, and even shopping lists). Plus, if you want to create a library for yourself, and for the family, you can do that. Even custom information is important, such as the traffic route for one person to get to where they need to go. Seating up profiles is essential in using this great system. How do you do this though? Well, you're about to find out.

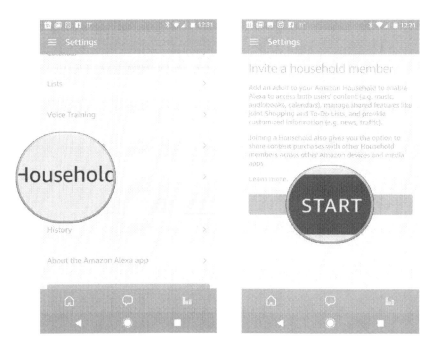

## Adding Users

Now, to add anyone to this, you have to follow just a few tips. You need to have everyone that's in your home present, both adults and children, and then, you can follow the settings needed.

First, you go to settings then accounts, and then choose the tab that says, "household profile." From there, you'll follow the instructions. You'll be asked to put the other people's account information on there, so pass it around so that they can all add to it.

But there are a few things that you will need to keep in mind. When you do have a second adult on there, they can use the cards associated with your account to make purchases. However, you can put a confirmation code there. Another thing that you should watch out is the fact that they can access the Prime photos. However, you can restrict access to the Echo Show.

Another thing to keep in mind is that on the Echo Look, you can only look at and delete the photos on the account, so there is more protection. Alexa will ask which account is the one being used, and then if you do ask to take a photo after switching or after 15 minutes, it will ask for the user.

## Help & Customer Service

Amazon Device Support › Amazon Echo Help › Amazon Alexa App ›

### Household Profiles on Alexa Devices

| Q Search Help | Go |

‹ All Help Topics

Amazon Echo Help

With Household Profiles, you can add another adult to your Amazon Household to listen to either users' content (for example, music and audiobooks) and manage shared features (for example, lists).

Joining a Household also gives you the option to share certain content purchases with other Household members across other Amazon devices and media apps.

**Note:** When you add a second adult to your Household, you are authorizing the other adult to use credit cards associated with your Amazon account for purchases on Amazon. You may require a 4-digit code to say aloud when you confirm purchases with your credit card. To require a confirmation code, select **Settings** in the Alexa app, and then select **Voice Purchasing**.

Download the Amazon Alexa App
Amazon Alexa App Basics
Amazon Alexa App Settings
Household Profiles on Alexa Devices
Voice Training
Turn On Alexa Skills
Send Feedback About Alexa
View Your Dialog History

### Add a User to Your Household

1. Make sure the person you invite to your Household is present.
2. From the left navigation panel in the Alexa app, select **Settings**.
3. Select **Household profiles**.
4. Follow the instructions for the second person to join your Amazon Household. During the process, pass your phone, tablet, or laptop to the second person to enter their account information.

## Switching profiles

One thing that you might want to know more about, is how to switch profiles. Once you set up the household, how you switch accounts is simple. When you want to switch accounts, you can say "Alexa, switch accounts." To verify that you're using the correct account, you can even ask "Alexa, whose account is this?" and you'll get an answer for that. If you're doing it on the app, you use the menu at the top of the screen to toggle between the libraries.

Adults in Jason's Household

Jason Fitzpatrick                          Leave

███████ Fitzpatrick                       Remove

## Removing a user

Sometimes, if you're using an Alexa device in a house where someone might want to move out, you'll need to remove their profile. If you do need to remove an adult, you're not able to add it to the same account, or to another account, for about 180 days, so make sure that's what you want to do before you do it. If it's done by accident and you want to re-add it, you can contact customer service. To remove this is simple, and you just have to go to the settings tab in the Alexa app.

From there, you go to accounts once again, and then you can choose "In an Amazon household with (name specified)" and from there, you can choose to remove the user that you want to get rid of. If you're removing yourself, you can choose to leave. It'll prompt you again, so if you for sure want to do this, you can press it again in order to confirm the change that you're making.

Sometimes you need to know how to add and remove profiles from your home. This chapter gave you the know-how on how to do this, and you'd be surprised just how useful this is for yourself, and why you should definitely have this knowledge if you're planning on using this device.

## 18 Chapter – How to Get Alexa to Start Your Day

Did you know that you could use Alexa to kickstart your day? With this, you can pre-program various commands into Alexa to go off at a certain time, or even with a certain command. It's great, but there are a few limits to this. It kicks off at a time or a command that you choose, but in order for this to work, it has to be something that isn't music related, because at this time, you can't include the music player command. However, there are still some great uses for this, allowing you to begin your day, and let's face it, having a routine makes this better.

Now, with the new Echo system, you can enable alarms on it as well, which is super helpful. There are constant updates being made to this, with new features being installed, so it's possible that there will be more additions to this as time goes on.

Right now, you can use news, flash briefing, weather, traffic, or a smart home device. Essentially, it's a way to set up flash briefing to wake up to, and you can add some extra tidbits of information and turn off devices and such, or turn them on when you wake up. It'll get updates though, so hopefully it'll allow music in the future. Currently, if you want to add any feedback, you can go to the help and feedback area of the Alexa app to tell Amazon what they should add. They do listen. They'll work with this.

But, it's not an end-all to the system. In fact, it still allows this to work like a charm, and here is how you use it.

**How to set up Alexa Routines so it's actually useful.**

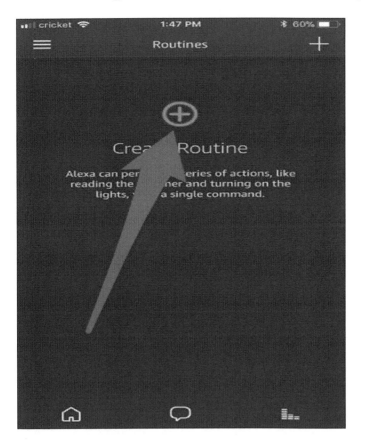

Now, here is how you set it up so that you can get some use out of it. Essentially, you want to go to the main menu of the app, which is that hamburger icon that's located at the top of the screen. It's called that because of the horizontal lines looking almost like a hamburger. Now, you can then when you have the menu open go to a variety of functions, but this time around, we're going to Routines.

Once the Routine option is opened up, you'll see the "start my day" setup as the default option, but of course, this isn't enabled. To enable this, you can tap the icon that's next to it to review it, edit the start time or even the command, and then enable it. To add more routines, you can press the plus icon and then you will set it up as you go along.

Now, once you press the plus button, you will see the routine that's pictured below. Essentially, this is what Alexa will do the second the "trigger" that's stated begins. Currently, there are only two triggers that you can use, the command that you've spoken and specified, or even the scheduled time. If you're the type that wants to say good morning to Alexa before you begin, you'll say "Alexa, good morning" or "Alexa, good night," and that will trigger the command. If you want Alexa to wake you up with a flash briefing, you use the time instead, and that is how it'll wake the system. Now, if you want to, you can press the plus button to change either of these.

Now, the "when this happens" is essentially what will be said to trigger the action. The "Add action" is what action will be done the second either the phrase is uttered or the time. If you want to maybe disable the security system, so long as it's connected to your Alexa system, the add action can be "disable security system" or if you're saying, "Alexa, good night" you can with this action shut down the Alexa system so that it sleeps, and also, turn off all the lights, and even lock your home up. It's pretty weird all that you can do with this.

Now, once you have all of this together, you then will create this.

Now, if you're struggling with what you want the action to be, you'll be given four options to choose from. They are news, traffic, smart home, and weather. There isn't much to be added just yet, but then, you can press one, and then you'll be given various options for each of these routine choices.

Once that's done, you'll be able to then have a routine set up, which is pretty good.

Now, currently it's lacking in some functions, which kind of stinks, and might be a limitation that many aren't into, for the sole reason that they want to have that extra addition. But, considering the fact that the Echo spot is being seen as a bedside alarm clock, it will definitely roll out these additions once it's released.

The Echo spot, in case you don't know, is an Alexa system that essentially looks like an alarm clock, meaning that it will function like one. However, it's got a lot of the Echo Show capabilities to it, which is one of the major benefits of it, since you can have the screen there. It's much smaller, but it does the job well, and it's a good one to have if you're considering getting another Echo device for your room.

This chapter went over the routines option and while it is lacking at this point, it's certainly something to consider if you want to start putting together a better routine using the Alexa system.

# 19 Chapter – Other Features

It might seem like we've covered everything Alexa could possibly do—after all, this book has already talked about a lot of options, from organizing your life to turning on your lights and heat. There are some capabilities, though, that don't fit into any other categories but that are still very useful to you in designing and running your smart home—and your life.

There are a lot of surprising devices that offer Alexa integration already on the market, and even more are likely to emerge as the technology develops further. These new options are rarely cheap when they first become available to consumers. As an example, the Samsung Family Hub Fridge has a touchscreen that gives you the option of communicating directly with Alexa in your kitchen—but will set you back between $5,000 and $6,000, about twice the cost of a comparable fridge without this capability.

From your yard and garden to the car in your garage, you can really use Alexa anywhere in your house, and for an impressive array of tasks. For some of these more esoteric offerings of the Alexa voice control program, check out the options in the chapter below.

## Transportation

There aren't many features yet that can be integrated into your car, but there are a few options that you'll find exceptionally helpful. The **Automatic** is a small device that you can connect to any car's diagnostic port and is incredibly affordable considering its capabilities, only setting you back around $100.

The Automatic uses Bluetooth to communicate with Alexa and can give you information on your fuel level or the status of your engine, including lights denoting that you need an oil change, a tune-up on your engine, or a replacement of filters within your system. You can also use the Automatic to ask Alexa where you parked your car—very helpful when you're in a large garage or parking lot and don't want to waste time wandering up and down the aisles.

There is also a WiFi-enabled device called **Garageio** that synchs to Alexa and lets you use voice control in your garage. You can connect up to three garage doors into the Garageio system. Once they're connected, you can use voice commands through Alexa to open and close the doors remotely.

There are some cars that come equipped with Alexa integration, as well. The newest version of the Ford Sync infotainment system—which comes included on most of Ford's recent car models—gives you the full range of Alexa capabilities you have on your Echo, along with some driving-specific features similar to those offered by the automatic.

Even if you don't have a car—or can't use it at the moment—you can use Alexa to arrange your transportation. Integrate with your Uber account using an IFTTT recipe and you can ask Alexa to order you a ride, check out how far away the car is, or even cancel the trip if you decide you don't need it after all.

## Yard and garden

Your smart home can extend into the out of doors thanks to Alexa. You can use it to control any lights that are within the range of your WiFi network, including lights that are used in your back yard, around your pool or deck, or on your front porch. Most smart bulbs are not durable enough to withstand outdoor weather conditions, but you can use a smart plug or switch to let you control the standard outdoor bulbs strung up around your porch or yard.

You can also synch your sprinkler system into the rest of your smart home. The **Rachio** brand of sprinkler systems is the first to offer Alexa integration. Using it, you can control the areas of your sprinkler system, set how they respond to different weather conditions and levels of precipitation, or turn them on and off manually with a command.

If you don't have a Rachio system installed but you'd like Alexa to help you out in your yard and garden, check out the **GreenIQ Smart Garden Hub.** This is a WiFi compatible sprinkler controller that interacts with local weather stations and plant sensors to help you manage your outdoor domain. The Smart Garden Hub controls both sprinklers and outdoor lighting, and can even track your water consumption, helping you to save money on your utility bills.

**Telephone lines**

It might seem strange that technology as advanced as Alexa would be compatible with something seemingly archaic, like a land line, but thanks to the company **Ooma Telo** you can revolutionize the concept of the home phone, bringing it into the 21st century.

Ooma Telo is an impressive home phone program that lets you place phone calls over the internet, giving you free nationwide calling for around $100-$150. Once you integrate it with Alexa, you can make calls and get information on missed or incoming calls with a simple voice command.

# 20 Chapter – The Echo's Most Recently Added Skills

## August Home Skill

With the new August Home Skill for Alexa, you can now use your voice to lock your doors or check the status of your door locks in the house. To use this skill, you will need an August Lock and an August Connect Hub. To order these items just say, "Alexa, order August Lock" or "Alexa, order August Connect." Once you've set up and named these devices on the Echo, go to *Skills* in your Alexa app to enable the August Home Skill and link your account.

## Election Skill

The new *Washington Post* Election Skill can keep you up-to-date on the race to the White House by getting poll data and tapping into a daily politics brief. To enable this skill just go to the *Skills* section of your Alexa app, and say, "Alexa, ask WaPo Elections for the Politics Brief" or "Alexa, ask WaPo Elections for the polls."

## Skills by Category

The Alexa app has been redesigned and you can now view skills by category, which makes it even easier to locate and enjoy Alexa skills. Now you can also see what's popular and trending. Alexa is amazing with more than 1,500 skills that include everything from ordering a Domino's pizza, getting an Uber ride, or even checking your Capital One credit card balance.

**PGA Tour Skill**

Alexa has a new PGA Tour Skill where you can track your favorite golfers with up-to-the-minute information and check the latest standings. Go to *Skills* in the Alexa app to enable the PGA Tour Skill and then just say, "Alexa, ask PGA Tour how Phil Mickelson is doing" or "Alexa, ask PGA Tour for the leader board."

**Sprinkler Skill**

Alexa has a new Rachio Sprinkler Skill where you can "say it and spray it." The Rachio sprinkler controller can turn the water on and off or delay a scheduled watering. Go to *Skills* in your Alexa app, enable the Rachio Sprinkler Skill and link your Rachio account. Then just say, "Alexa, ask Rachio to start zone 3 for 10 minutes" or "Alexa, ask Rachio to delay zone 5 for 10 minutes."

**Amazon Package Tracking**

Now you can track your Amazon packages with Alexa. You don't need your phone or computer because Alexa can tell you when your next package will arrive. She can also tell you when your order was placed and add a link to more details in your Alexa app. Just ask "Alexa, where's my stuff?" or say, "Alexa, track my order."

**Calendar Events**

Alexa can now add calendar events directly to your Google Calendar just by using your voice. This makes it even easier to manage your daily schedule. In your Alexa app, go to *Settings* and then tap *Calendar*. Once you are set up, simply say, "Alexa, add vet visit with Milo to my calendar."

## Plan Your Weekends By Asking Alexa Questions About Specific Events

You can now ask Alexa about movie show times at theaters near you. With information about films currently in theaters, let Alexa help you plan your weekends. To use this new feature just say, "Alexa, tell me about the movie, *The Revenant*," or "Alexa, what movies are playing on Saturday night?"

## BMW's New Mind-Blowing Partnership With Amazon Echo

BMW announced plans to let people connect their vehicle to Amazon Echo. This functionality is scheduled to be available by the end of this year. BMW owners will then be able to use voice commands to do things like lock their vehicle's doors or check their vehicle's fuel level.

The BMW company is creating a new Amazon Echo skill that will give BMW owners the ability to control their car with Echo. This specific feature is actually part of the company's grand effort to bring more connectivity to its cars.

BMW's new cloud-based technology platform, released in March, is called BMW Connected and will offer various new services to BMW owners.

## "Alexa, Find Me A Job"

I think we would all agree that job searches can be

exhausting. There is endless typing, reading, and searching Google and other job sites. Now you can find a job through Alexa using the ZipRecruiter app. The mundane experience of job searching is one reason why ZipRecruiter developed an Echo app that encourages people to say, "Alexa, find me a job." This ZipRecruiter app allows job seekers to ask Alexa what jobs are available, details about the position(s), and allows users to apply to them if they have a resume on file with ZipRecruiter.

At the moment, Echo owners can only hear about and apply to jobs with the ZipRecruiter app, but the plan is to build more features in the coming months. Future functionality of ZipRecruiter and Alexa could include listing a job of the day, creating a resume, and answering interview questions.

## Touchscreen Video Device

The new Nucleus touchscreen device is the first of its kind to connect with Alexa. The Nucleus touchscreen device is approximately 9 inches by 7 inches and just 2.1 pounds, roughly the size of a tablet. The paired touchscreen video screens and embedded cameras can be accessed via an app on your smart phone to allow communication with any room in your home that is equipped with a Nucleus Device.

# 21 Chapter – Grouping Your Smart Home Devices

Using your Amazon Echo and Echo Dot with your smart home devices is a major game changer for the Echo and Echo Dot. Therefore, grouping your devices together makes it easier to control multiple devices and multiple rooms at once is essential.

Within the Alexa application you are able to create a group of smart home devices that will give you the ability to control multiple smart home devices all at once.

### *How to create a Smart Home Group on Your Echo*

From your mobile device open the Alexa mobile application. Locate Smart Home from your left navigation panel in the Alexa app.

Select the term Groups from the menu > Create Groups.

Enter your anticipated group name. Room names are

generally used to give your group a recognizable name. For example, in order to group every smart item connected in the bedroom, simply name your group mastered.

Once the group has been named you now have the ability to select the devices in which you would like to add to this group. Select Add once you are complete.

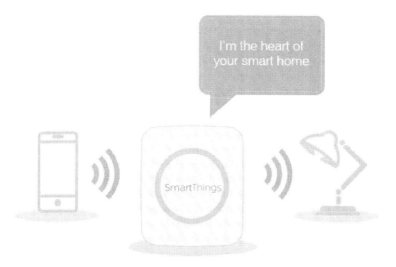

Once your group has been created in the Alexa app you are now able to use commands via Alexa with it. For some skills you may need to tell Alexa to "Open [skill name]" before your request can be recognized and completed. Sample commands to be used with your smart home devices may include the following:

*"Turn on [Smart Device Name or group]"*

*"Set [Group Name] to [#]%"*

Your device scene can be managed through the desired device's companion application. Scene names are shown in the Smart Home section of the Alexa application.

Smart Groups can also be edited within the Alexa

Application. This can be done under Groups, simply by selecting the group you would like to edit. You would make changes to the name by selecting the desired group and editing the text information. In order to change the items within the group, select or de select the checkbox next to the application. Lastly, in order to delete the grouping simply select Delete.

## 22 Chapter – The Limitations of Alexa

One of the most common problems an Alexa user experiences, even those who love the product, is that each command must be voiced separately. For instance, unless you have created a group called "living room and bedroom," you cannot say "Alexa, turn on the living room and bedroom lights." Each command will have to be stated separately as "Alexa, turn on the living room lights" and then "Alexa, turn on the bedroom light." You can only directly address individual devices or groups in Alexa, even if you've created scenes, routines, or robots in the smart home hub app.

Likewise, when creating a shopping list, you must add each item separately. For instance, you can't say "Alexa, add milk and eggs to my shopping list." The appropriate commands are "Alexa, add milk to my shopping list," then "Alexa, add eggs to my shopping list." A large shopping list can make this process annoying for both the user and anyone else in the room.

Alexa creates a shopping list in its app that you can access while in the grocery store. However, if you are asking someone else to do the shopping from this list who doesn't have access to your Alexa app, you will need to use an IFTTT applet to create a version of the list for sharing or printing.

If you own multiple Alexa devices and have them in different rooms, you could experience problems as a result of the limited amount of wake words. You can change the wake word for each device, but the only options currently available are "Alexa," "Amazon," or "Echo." If you are in one room but are still in ear shot of a device in another room, it is likely that both devices will respond if they have the same wake word. However, if you have different wake words for each device it could get confusing remembering which word works with which individual device.

Although Amazon has built-in noise cancellation technology, it sometimes doesn't respond due to music playing too loud or background noise in the room. Also, if one person says the wake word and someone else in the room says "pass me the ketchup," you may receive an off-the-wall response from Alexa. Though it is an occasional problem, Alexa is still a better listener than some of my friends or family. Periodically, Amazon will send automatic firmware updates. Performance changes after these updates have been reported as sometimes causing improvement and sometimes not. Unfortunately, you cannot control when these updates arrive.

Although the Amazon Echo is boasted as a Bluetooth speaker, if you use it primarily for music, you shouldn't expect a whole house music system. Though your Echo can play music in every room, because the stream to each speaker is independent, they can't synchronize the way a whole house music system can. You are required to go to each Alexa device and tell it to play music separately. You cannot tell one device to "play music on all my speakers," for instance. Since Amazon Prime's music rule only allows one stream at a time, you'll need to use another music service in other rooms.

Alexa may disappoint if you use TuneIn for podcasts. A voice search for a particular podcast or episode can also be frustrating. Also, don't be surprised if TuneIn stations become temporarily unavailable.

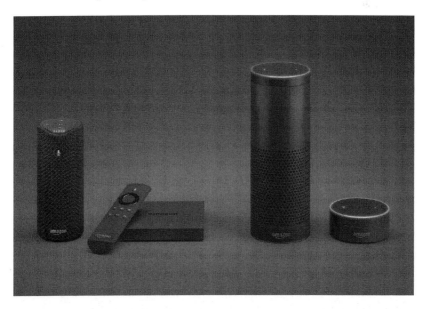

## 23 Chapter – Google Home Vs. Amazon Echo

When comparing the Amazon Echo and the Google Home, the clear winner should be obvious. The Amazon Echo originally signified the beginning of a virtual assistant era being that it was one of the first products in its class. The original Echo's success brought on the introduction of the Amazon Echo and the Amazon Echo Tap. These products essentially provided something for everyone. The various types appealed to a variety of audiences while still staying true to the essential mission of the original Amazon Echo.

With success generally comes imitation. The Google Home was brought to the public in October of 2016. Google Home performs similarly to the Google Assistant on a smart phone.

The Amazon Echo products and the Google Home differ in a variety of ways. The most obvious difference is the price of the device.

The original Amazon Echo is priced at 179 while the Google Home is priced at 129. Both devices require either an

Android or IOS operating system. However, the Google Home has specific version requirements. The Amazon Echo is also compatible with Fire OS and accessible via your computer's web browser.

There are a number of distinctions between the Google Home & the Amazon Echo these differences will be highlighted later on in this chapter.

Google Home has been described as "a voice-activated speaker powered by the Google Assistant." The Google Home is built to rival the Amazon Echo and its smart home functionalities. It is able to control household items like temperature or lights. Google, which is known for its search functionality, brought the Google Home into existence.

If you regularly use Google Calendar, Google Maps or any Google run applications the Google Home may be an admirable option. It would not be uncommon to find that individuals might like a device that readily integrates with technology that they are already utilizing.

The Amazon Echo allows users to a variety of items that normal do not operate in the hands free realm. The voice control of the Amazon Echo gives users unique abilities and conveniences. The Amazon Echo is not only designed to be a smart home hub it is also designed to play music via a variety of streaming services.

The Amazon Echo and the Google Home both have a sophisticated look. They are both suitable for almost any location but would look best on a shelving unit.

The Amazon Echo resembles a small black tower. The Amazon Echo like the other Alexa Suite of products has seven microphones, so it easily picks up sound from any direction. The Google Home is shaped like a small vase, which resembles an air freshener with a swappable base. The base can swap for a variety of colors that match your environment.

*Google Home vs. Amazon Echo*

| | | |
|---|---|---|
| Price | $130 | $180 |
| Responds to voice commands | Yes | Yes |
| Always listening | Yes | Yes |
| Wake word | Okay Google or Hey Google | Alexa, Echo, or Amazon |
| Music streaming options | Google Play Music, YouTube Music, Spotify, Pandora, TuneIn | Amazon Prime Music, Spotify, Pandora, iHeartRadio, TuneIn, others |

| | | |
|---|---|---|
| Smart home partnerships | Nest, SmartThings, Philips Hue, Belkin WeMo, Honeywell, IFTTT | Nest, Ecobee, Honeywell, SmartThings, Wink, Insteon, Belkin WeMo, Philips Hue, Lifx, Big Ass Fans, IFTTT, Control4, Crestron, other devices via skills |
| Customizable appearance | Yes | No |
| Output to stereo system | Yes, via Chromecast | No (yes with Amazon ) |
| Synced audio playback to multiple devices | Yes, to any Google Cast device | No |
| Personal assistant highlights | Search Google, get a personalized daily briefing, check traffic, check your calendar, make a shopping list, check flight status, track a package | Add items to calendar, make a shopping list, make a to do list, check flight status, track a package |
| Other features | Cast to your TV with Chromecast, launch and control YouTube or Netflix via Chromecast | Order a pizza, play a game, arrange an Uber pickup. Echo has an ever-growing list of thousands of skills and counting |

Chart taken from CNET.com

# Conclusion

Alexa is a great piece of hardware that can be used to help you get the most out of your personal assistant and control of your own home. It's remarkable all that it can do, and you can reap the benefits of this as soon as you begin to use it. It's amazing all that Alexa is capable of, and you too can work with Alexa to control your home, make it easier, and use these new tips and tricks that have recently been updated to make your life easier.

Alexa is constantly being updated, with new and amazing techniques and tricks that can be used to help make navigating it easier. Plus, with the creation of skills and the like, you too can get the most that you can out of it, and even make skills that nobody has ever heard of. You can then put it in the skills store, and people will be able to use these, which in turn will help to make your Alexa system more personal for you.

So yes, you can use Alexa in many different ways, and this book gave you some of the helpful tips that you can try out in order to get the most out of this. Your next step is to use Alexa, to get the benefits that you know are there, and actually start to master this system. It's fun, and there are so many cool tips and tricks out there, that you don't want to miss them.

Thanks for buying the book!

Made in the USA
Middletown, DE
26 December 2017